THE Artist IN THE OFFICE

How to creatively Survive and Thrive
Seven Days a week

Summer Pierre

A Perigee Book

For Julie
FORMER BOSS, FABULOUS LADY

A PERIGEE BOOK
Published by the Penguin Group
Penguin Group (USA) Inc.
375 Hudson Street, New York, New York 10014, USA
Penguin Group (Canada), 90 Eglinton Avenue East, Suite 700, Toronto, Ontario M4P 2Y3, Canada (a division of Pearson Penguin Canada Inc.) • Penguin Books Ltd., 80 Strand, London WC2R 0RL, England • Penguin Group Ireland, 25 St. Stephen's Green, Dublin 2, Ireland (a division of Penguin Books Ltd.) • Penguin Group (Australia), 250 Camberwell Road, Camberwell, Victoria 3124, Australia (a division of Pearson Australia Group Pty. Ltd.) • Penguin Books India Pvt. Ltd., 11 Community Centre, Panchsheel Park, New Delhi—110 017, India • Penguin Group (NZ), 67 Apollo Drive, Rosedale, North Shore 0632, New Zealand (a division of Pearson New Zealand Ltd.) • Penguin Books (South Africa) (Pty.) Ltd., 24 Sturdee Avenue, Rosebank, Johannesburg 2196, South Africa
Penguin Books Ltd., Registered Offices: 80 Strand, London WC2R 0RL, England

While the author has made every effort to provide accurate telephone numbers and Internet addresses at the time of publication, neither the publisher nor the author assumes any responsibility for errors, or for changes that occur after publication. Further, the publisher does not have any control over and does not assume any responsibility for author or third-party websites or their content.

First edition: February 2010

Library of Congress Cataloging-in-Publication Data

Pierre, Summer, 1972–
   The artist in the office : how to creatively survive and thrive seven days a week / Summer Pierre.—A Perigee book.
      p. cm.
   ISBN 978-0-399-53564-2
   1. Artists—Psychology. 2. Arts—Vocational guidance. 3. Creation (Literary, artistic, etc.) 4. Quality of work life. I. Title.
   NX165.P53 2010
   702.3—dc22   2009039554

PRINTED IN THE UNITED STATES OF AMERICA

10 9 8 7 6 5 4 3 2

Most Perigee books are available at special quantity discounts for bulk purchases for sales promotions, premiums, fund-raising, or educational use. Special books, or book excerpts, can also be created to fit specific needs. For details, write: Special Markets, Penguin Group (USA) Inc., 375 Hudson Street, New York, New York 10014.

Contents

THE ARTIST IN THE OFFICE:
AN INTRODUCTION

WHY WE WORK

Part 2

YOUR ARTIST AT WORK

DOING YOUR WORK

Part 4

IDEAS FOR CHANGE

TO BE NOBODY-BUT-
YOURSELF-- IN A WORLD
WHICH IS DOING ITS
BEST, NIGHT AND DAY, TO
MAKE YOU EVERYBODY
ELSE - MEANS TO FIGHT
THE HARDEST BATTLE
WHICH ANY HUMAN BEING
CAN FIGHT, AND NEVER
STOP FIGHTING.

— e.e. cummings

THE Artist IN THE OFFICE
∽ — An Introduction — ∽

Day after day, this is how it goes: We get up, we get ready, and we go to work. We don't ask why, we just do it. Then we spend our time at work in a sort of conscious slumber—we lose days to activities that sometimes don't have meaning to us. Suddenly, we wake up and realize eight hours or five days or whatever time is gone, and we can't account for it. As a society we somehow accept that the majority of how we spend our lives will be like this. We save our living for after 5:00 p.m. and weekends or holidays. We save our *real* selves for the cracks and corners of our off time. We think we have to do this in order to survive, but what do we do to actually *live*?

As an artist, I have always felt I was living two lives—my "day job life" and my "real life" as an active artist. I resented going to work and tried to make it work for me as much as I could: As a musician, I used my vacation time for touring; I touted my gigs to coworkers. I performed at office Christmas parties. As an illustrator, I drew more birthday, graduation, baby shower, and wedding shower cards for my office mates to sign than I care to count. In the meantime, I sneaked in mailers and posters through the copy machines and Internet outlets. I wrote short stories and novel chapters in the margins

of time I found throughout the day. I thought until I "made it" I didn't have a choice. "Making it" meant fame, the ability to do art full-time, or both. Until then, I wasn't a *real* artist. As a result, I felt ashamed and invisible next to the full-time artists I idolized, and angry and invisible next to the people who enjoyed their jobs. I wasn't a real employee and I wasn't a real artist. No wonder I felt so screwed!

I have recognized this same scenario in the faces of published writers who still hold down jobs, in painters with solo gallery shows who wait tables at night, and in crafters who sew late into the night so they can mail an order in the morning. There is a sense that, as artists with day jobs, we aren't quite "legit."

As it happens many "legit" artists also had day jobs. The poet Walt Whitman was a teacher and a nurse. Even Georgia O'Keeffe, painter and American icon, worked as a teacher initially. The writer Charles Bukowski worked as a postal clerk. I can tell you that when Charles Bukowski was asked at a party, "So what do you do?" He never answered, "Postal clerk." He was always a real writer front and center.

What Are You Front & Center?

As with these famous examples, we working artists have day jobs for various reasons. Maybe we can't imagine another way; maybe it's temporary until we hit the big time; maybe we like health insurance and a place to go—but the reality is *we work two jobs*. As writers who wait tables, actresses who work office jobs, painters who are teachers, and artists who work as executives, we artists with day jobs juggle the job that puts food on our table and the job that feeds us. This is no small effort!

This little book isn't about not working, it's about acknowledging the work we do. It's about waking up in the life we inhabit *now* instead of putting off life for *later*. Inside you will find new ways to look at your job and daily life so that you can live more of what you want and less of what you don't. We will also explore how to stay creative and motivated during any given workday (including things to do while you are at work), and how to focus and get your creative work done while keeping a job as well as your sanity. And just because it's the elephant in the living room, we will also explore the exciting world of money, ideas for changing your job, and so much more! *The Artist in the Office* can help you *thrive* both at your creative work and at your day job. It may seem like you are living two lives, but I assure you: It is one life only—and it's yours. Why not enjoy it all?

And just in case you're in doubt, I want to let you in on a secret that writer David Sedaris once inscribed to me in one of his books:

We are! Now let's go!

A Slave No More

Once, at a party, I was asked the inevitable question: "So, what do you do?" I replied that I was an artist. After we covered exactly what "artist" meant, my new acquaintance asked me, "So, do you do that full-time, or are you just a wage slave?"

I hate the term "wage slave." To me, it implies a sort of victim relationship to having a job. It's as if, as artists, we are shackled to our regular paychecks. This is utter crap. Nobody pointed a gun to my head and said, "March into that job interview, make a good impression, and take the job." No matter what I'd rather do or not do, I made a choice to go after my day job. I'm also paid for it.

Often when we dream about being somewhere else—as in a full-time creative life—we can come to resent where we are and think of ourselves as victims or slaves to the system.

Break the wage slave mentality. Make empowering work choices and acknowledge your worth!

One time, when I was nervous about a job interview, my brother Blake said:

This reminds me that I am providing a service and my time is valuable.

YOUR TIME IS VALUABLE!

The Truth About Jobs

I have never had a job where employees didn't have an ongoing list of complaints. It seems to be the nature of work life. The management is lousy or the employees are underappreciated or they are just bored out of their minds. But here is the reality:

Your job is not the problem.

For me, I always believed my job was the problem. I was an artist and I hated having a job, but I didn't know how else to live. I tried different kinds of jobs: art store clerk, nanny, and administrative assistant in various atmospheres. I tried to get a job in something I believed in—helping the poor—and I was still bored and angry. I tried getting a job working with kids—ditto the experience. I decided I needed more money, so I got a job at a wealthy foundation—still frustrated beyond measure. It finally dawned on me that it didn't matter how much money I was being paid, or what kind of environment I was in, it was still *me* coming to work: depressed, sarcastic, adolescent me. I realized if anything was going to change, it had to start with me.

So I tried to quit working cold turkey—a few times—and something interesting happened.

I didn't do so well.

The magical life I thought being a full-time artist would entail dissolved the moment my coffee mug was empty. I was still bored, still scared out of my mind, only I was lonelier than ever. I still felt disempowered and like a victim of circumstance or of my own poor childhood or of whatever thing I could think of. Also, and more important, I got just about as much art done as I did when I was working full-time. I was still me and I was *baffled as hell*.

It turned out there were a lot of things that having a job did for me. At a minimum, it gave me structure, accountability, and an opportunity to be around people.

If we are dissatisfied with work, we think: "If only I could win the lottery and not work, that would solve all my problems" or "I wish I could just work from home." But the truth is, work, like anything else, is a relationship that requires our own participation. I assure you that if you didn't have to go to a job every day, you would have a whole set of other issues that would come up. Consider how you are participating in your own job relationship. How do you show up? If your job really is the problem then *get out now*. When you get another job, just check and see if the same issues keep coming up. Are you still bored, angry, frustrated with your bosses and the management? These things happen everywhere—that doesn't make them right, but ask yourself what is going to change with me?

Before we can find our ideal work environment, we must find out what about work works for us. There are a lot of reasons that we work for jobs, but have you ever considered how a job works for you?

The Tale of the Crappy Job
(and How It still Worked)

Years ago I worked at a cheapskate natural foods company, which paid its employees a low hourly wage, gave us a minimum of sick days and holidays, and had us working in ancient trailers. They provided health insurance, but the co-pay was so high that no one could afford to go to the doctor. Like most dysfunctional jobs, the management was a nightmare. I dreaded going to work and complained about it daily. It was easy and fun to bitch about. There was *so much* material!

Why did I stay there at all? When I took stock of what this job *actually* provided for me, it was quite a lot: All the healthy snack food I could enjoy; a five-minute walk to the Pacific Ocean (I once saw a school of dolphins on my lunch hour—it was magical!); if my car was in the shop, I could borrow a car from sales. Because they also had their own distribution company, they helped me ship my sixty pounds of books from the East Coast. When I moved back they provided pallets to load all my things onto, and drove them to the movers a hundred miles away, free of charge. This also doesn't even touch on the fact that I sat next to my boss every day, a woman who ended up being an important friend and mentor. Call me Pollyanna, but there was a lot that *did* work for me.

Make a list of all the things your job actually provides for you—
be as specific as you can. Instead of "rent" say "two-bedroom
apartment, with colorful walls." Also include things that you
use or enjoy that come directly from being at the job. For me
that would include tea, coffee, hot chocolate, Internet service,
a social atmosphere, and the pen I am writing with.

you are provided for!

HOW WE SPEND OUR DAYS IS HOW WE SPEND OUR LIVES.

— ANNIE DILLARD

Idealizing

Much of my time on this planet has been about yearning for what I don't have. Like a lot of people, I have had an active fantasy life about how I wanted things to be, which left me resenting the way things actually were. When I was living this high-flying future life in my mind, it was a *total bummer* to wake up to where I *really* was. The yearning was making me blind to the ways I was already living parts of that dream.

A couple of years ago, when I first moved to New York, I was about to go on tour for the first time in years. I was on the phone with a friend, talking about the tour, and worrying about finding a job when I got back. I was deep into complaint mode (which just means I was afraid and feeling helpless). I was complaining about how I still needed a job and how I hadn't figured out how to make a living doing what I loved. "But," my wise friend said, "notice how you already are making a living doing what you love." It was at that moment that I realized she was right. For two weeks, I was going to be working full-time as a musician. Just because I had to get a job when I got back didn't mean those two weeks didn't count!

I started to look around and see other ways I was already living my dream life. I was living in New York, in an apartment I loved. I had a partner who tickled me silly, and an artist studio for the first time in my life.

Um, HELLO! This is REAL LIFE TALKING! Not too shabby!

As artists we all have running fantasy lives about our future glory. What do those fantasies contain? What are the ways you can live them right now? If you imagine yourself going to art school, how about paying a visit to that art school? If you're like me, you might have a fantasy about what you will do when you get your first book published. My fantasy was always to sign the large and extravagant book contract and then go to Boathouse Restaurant in Central Park. Until I got the large book contract, the Boathouse Restaurant seemed out of reach and something to enjoy only in my dreams. Then some friends surprised me by taking me there for dinner and it suddenly dawned on me: The Boathouse was available for dinner *now*. I didn't have to wait to go there—my life was special occasion enough!

Elements of your ideal life are happening right now and, in order for them to grow into the full picture, they just need encouragement.

TRY THIS

List all the ways you are already living your ideal life.

   Examples: I have two cats I adore, I wrote today, I wore a beautiful silk kimono, and I live in a town I love.

TRY THIS

What is one small step you can take today toward your ideal life?

   Examples: Drinking champagne with dinner, finding out the next open house for the art school of my dreams, drawing at lunchtime.

Moving Out of Why-I-Hate-Where-I-Workville (The True Dirt on Gossip)

I know it's *so fun* to dish. For me, it's like someone scratching a spot I can't get at. My leg practically thumps the floor with ecstasy when someone has a witty or sarcastic insight into someone or something at work. I love humor and stories, so I *love* good dirt. But here's the thing: Gossip really creates more shit than it purges. I know why it's done and why I do it. It's a way to connect with others in an often impersonal environment. It's also a cheap thrill and a way to somehow make sense of the insanity that the workplace can often breed. But I am here to tell you: This cure is part of the disease!

I can hear the collective cry of nearly every person I have worked with: "Don't take gossip away—that's all we have!"

The truth about gossip (or dishing or chronic complaining) is that it is often masked anger, expressed passive aggressively. No action comes from gossip. If you *really* want change, gossip won't help you—in fact, it will keep you running in place.

I once sat with two women who I worked with, talking about changes we wanted to make in our lives. We had met after work specifically for this purpose. Almost immediately the "work talk" started spinning its wheels. It was like a black hole of complaint we had unknowingly stepped into—the evidence of why we were all so wronged kept coming—and it was intoxicating! I caught us doing it—getting stuck in Why-I-Hate-Where-I-Workville, and I immediately jumped in and asked that we *limit* the complaining and bitching about work. It was preventing us from doing *anything*.

TRY THIS

Limit the bitching, gossiping, and complaining about work. When you find yourself tempted, ask yourself: "What am I angry about? What's *really* stuck in my craw?"

Maybe you're pissed that your boss was angry with you, maybe you feel stuck and bored, maybe you feel lonely. Most likely, your own sub-story (or your own dirt) is a lot more interesting! You can do more with it than just feel itchy.

Think I'm nuts? Try it for just one day . . . I dare you!

TRY THIS

Make a list of all the things you *like* about your job. I don't care where you work, there must be things that you like!

For me, some examples would be: my friend Jose, less worry about money, and the view of Manhattan.

A special NOTE TO ALL ADMINISTRATIVE, EXECUTIVE, and PERSONAL ASSISTANTS: YOUR JOB IS TO HELP SOMEONE ELSE LIVE THEIR DREAM. HOW ABOUT LENDING SOME OF THAT ENERGY AND SKILL TO YOUR DREAM?

YOU ARE QUALIFIED

Be of service. Go where you CAN help... If you're an artist, be of service to your art; don't have it the other way around. You have to put aside your dreams of being a hot shot and learn to be useful... You step up everyday, get a nice clean hit, and you're done.

—Cary Tennis

As an Artist You Are Always at Work

Part of my trouble when I was an employee involved attempting to leave the artist in me at home. What a crock! No wonder I was angry, bored, and distracted. It's a miracle that they got so much out of me at my jobs! I'd try to sneak my real life into my workday by surfing the Internet and complaining about "my plight." These are not bold acts of empowerment. These are passive-aggressive and often a junk-food kind of inspiration. They taste good, but don't get you to *do* anything.

One morning, I was getting ready for work, debating whether or not to carry my guitar on my commute. I had agreed to perform at a class after work, but, due to its bulk and size, my guitar case is a pain in the butt. In the end, I took it with me and once I stepped out my front door, something magical happened: I felt like me. Normally, when I traveled to work, I felt invisible—but carrying my guitar made me feel like I was carrying my real self—out into the world, and into work. It was powerful.

This experience taught me that as an artist I am always at work, and when I brought a physical tool of my artistry into the office, I felt more relaxed and alert. I was no longer divided between my real self and my work self. It changed my attitude—and it actually made me excited to come to work.

Make Work an Object of Your Creativity

One way to feel like you are bringing your artist to work is to experiment with creativity on the job.

Remember when you were a kid in school and you awoke during the week, wishing it was Saturday, only to remember that you had a field trip with your class planned that day? Remember the shift in your attitude? It was not your usual day! It was still school, but it was different. You were going on an adventure!

This is what an art project at work can do—it can shift your sense of going to work. Suddenly work isn't just your usual day at the desk, it's an adventure and an experiment. It's a place to explore and engage. Even something as small as making muffins or cookies and leaving them anonymously with a note can shift your attitude. You have a reason to be excited! Your job has become an object of your creativity.

What follows is a series of ideas to help you make work an object of your creativity. Once, an employer said to me, "If you don't know your options, you don't have any." Honey, if nothing else, let these exercises be a reminder that you have the option to make work a place for your creativity!

A WORD OF WARNING

(aka the fine print, the lowdown, the part where you go forward at your own risk!)

Do Your Job!

I'm not kidding. While I encourage you to do art projects and creative acts at work, the key is to do it *small*, so it doesn't get in the way of your actual job. Doing your job is the part that you agreed to do when you shook hands and accepted the paycheck. Keep up your end of the bargain and keep up your work. The creative acts I describe here are ways to keep your mind fresh and to change your experience at work, but you are responsible for getting your workload done efficiently and on time.

Know when you are pushing it and when it is not appropriate. Every work environment is different. I encourage you to create and live a full life away from and at the workplace, but if you get reprimanded or get any messages that this is not okay, know when to stop. (Also, know when to quit!)

Creative Commute

There are a lot of things you can do to shift your day by simply playing with your commute to work. A lot of people already do things like read books or magazines or listen to the radio or music. Most often, however, this is just a means to avoid boredom, and we don't notice when even these things become part of the mindless routine.

Trying something different in your commute, even for one day, can shift your perspective.

TRY THIS

* **Walking all or part of the commute.** Get up earlier and give yourself more time. Park far away from your job or get off early from the bus or subway. Experience the outside world before you go inside.

* **Listening to books on tape—this is also a shift in experience.** What is a subject you are interested in, or a book you've been meaning to read? Instead of reading it, how about listening to it? I listen to books on tape when I draw, because it occupies my critical mind while my artist mind is free to do its job. Consider also shifting your material. Do you always gravitate toward novels? How about listening to travel writing or mysteries or nonfiction?

* **Listening to music while walking, driving, or riding on a train is a well-known powerful creative tool.** Suddenly, your life is a movie, and it has the best soundtrack ever! If you get stuck in a rut with music, how about shaking things up with something new? The library is a great resource for checking out music and trying out a new genre.

* **Reading unusual books or magazines.** Why not art books or how-to books? What would be refreshing and light up your mind? Fashion, poetry, knitting, photography, fishing?

* **Doing guerilla art on the way to work.** Chalk messages or quotes on the sidewalk, or hide random art along the way. Make your commute a treasure map!

* **Recording your commute.** What does the morning commute sound like? Take a tape recorder or digital recorder with you.

* **Photographing your commute.** This is an act of paying attention and seeing your world. (Not recommended while driving!)

* **List making.** What was red on your commute? What was blue? How many people were using iPods? Create a game to play with a fellow commuter like subway bingo! Make a list of things to look for and whoever gets the first five things wins. This is a practice in being awake to your surroundings and paying attention.

Lunchtime Adventures

What about that law-given right of at least a half-hour break in the middle of the day? They made lunch breaks for a reason, but rarely do we use that time to its full capacity. We use lunch breaks to run errands, see the doctor or dentist, or (egads!) to sit at our desks and eat lunch while we surf the Internet or do more work. How about using it to actually nourish yourself? Think you don't have time for anything? In a five-day workweek, at half an hour a day, you could have a cumulative two and a half hours all to yourself! It's being wasted! There are *plenty* of lunchtime adventures to be had, whether it's simply going outside (aka away from your desk) to eat lunch or using it as time to play and feed your artistic soul.

A MESSAGE TO EMPLOYERS:

THINK IT'S NOT YOUR JOB TO CREATE A SUPPORTIVE AND STIMULATING ENVIRONMENT FOR EMPLOYEES? EMPLOYEES WHO ARE ACKNOWLEDGED AND HAPPY HAVE LESS ABSENTEEISM, FEWER HEALTH-RELATED ISSUES, AND ARE (MORE) PRODUCTIVE! MANY LARGE AND SUCCESSFUL COMPANIES HAVE LONG DISCOVERED THIS AS A CRUCIAL TOOL FOR THEIR GROWTH AND PROSPERITY.

SUPPORTING YOUR EMPLOYEES IS JUST GOOD BUSINESS!

YOUR TOOLS AT HAND

Office supplies = Art supplies

* DRAWING & WRITING UTENSILS *

SHARPIES

HIGHLIGHTER

PENCILS: (MECHANICAL & REGULAR)

ERASER

PENS: BALLPOINT, ROLLERBALL, MARKERS

WITE-OUT

CHALK
(guerrilla art's easiest & simplest tool — carry it with you wherever you go!)

* PAPER ACCESSORIES *

FILE FOLDERS

Envelopes
(IN VARIOUS SIZES)

great for sending out manuscripts to publishers, agents, readers, etc.

organize your own files! ALSO a great surface for drawing & painting!

✳ Paper - and all its glory! ✳

regular 8½ x 11

legal 8½ x 14

Folded in ½ it makes a great zine or book size!

Colored paper

Note cards

CARD STOCK great for covers

Postcards, drawings, novels, zines, comic books, journals, art books, letters, collages, fliers, posters, INVITATONS, CARDS, SIGNS, ETC.

I hope they never discontinue the stuff

W-OUT

STICKIES (POST ITS) come in various colors - create notes, mini-art, etc.

TAPE (CLEAR)

MASKING

BINDERS FOR NOVELS, POETRY, MISC. WRITINGS, OR WHATEVER PROJECT AT HAND!

my DAMN NOVEL WHAT'S IT TO YOU?

Hole puncher

glue stick

great for journaling, collages, evidence collecting!

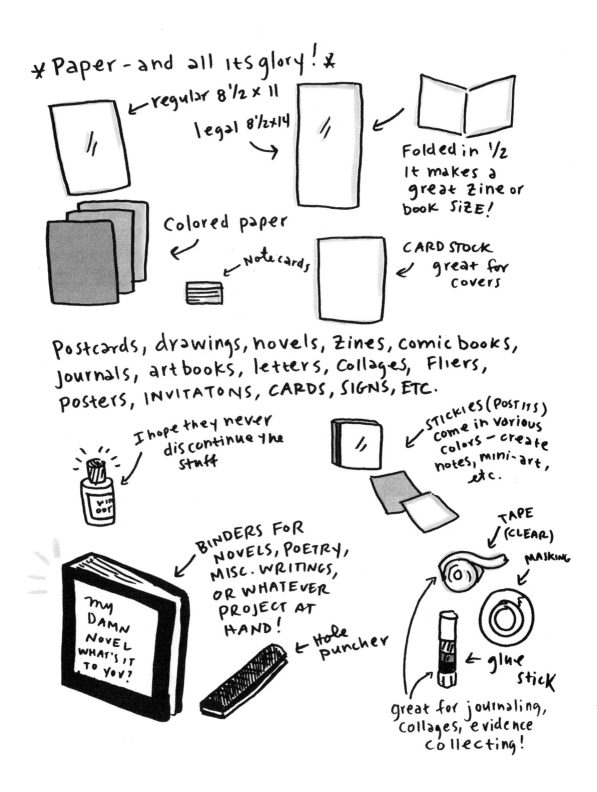

Find someone at work, preferably someone just as bored as you. Every time you see each other, start to dance.

EVIDENCE - WORK · 5/20/07

HOPEFULLY.

1 of 2 rubberbands floating around on my desk.

A DIME from .15¢ That has been there forever.

MICHAEL COHEN FOUND THIS on the street in SoHo, handed it to me and said "Lucky you." Apparently, I took it out of a pocket because I found it underneath some paper. Lucky me.

STICKIE

STAPLE FROM A greensheet I had to re-do the first page of.

CHOCOLATE I ate today

Phone message

coffee

Leaf from the florist shop downstairs

Ginger B.

Oregon

U. of Oregon

Collect the Evidence

For one day, collect evidence of everything you do.

YOU WILL NEED:

journal, notebook, or sketchbook
clear tape and/or glue
pen or pencil

As you go through your day, take small items you find in and around your desk and work area, like the lint from your rug or a paper clip you find on the floor, and tape or glue them to your notebook or journal page. Label each item. Feel free to spill coffee, test a pen, tear a piece from a memo—anything that acts as a small piece of your day. Date your evidence page. Do it as often as desired.

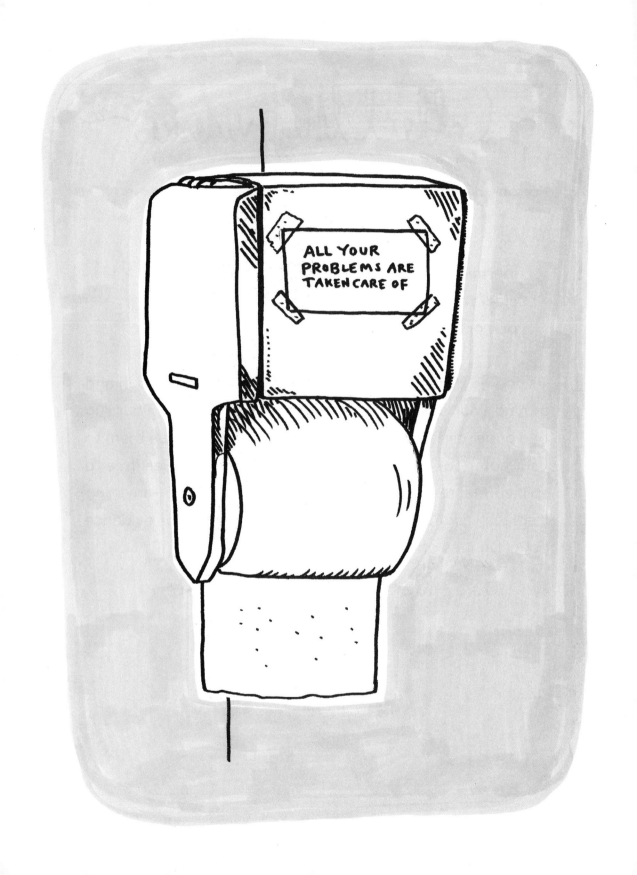

Be a Secret Messenger for Good

Take hopeful, inspirational, motivational, positive messages and/or quotes, and put them in secret places around your office.

Examples: inside cabinets, on whiteboards or flip charts, and inside bathroom stalls.

YOU WILL NEED:

paper and pen, or computer and printer

tape

Some Examples of Phrases and Quotes

All Your Problems Are Taken Care Of

Keep Up the Good Work

This Moment Is More Important Than You Think

How alive are you willing to be? —Anne Lamott

You are always on your way to a miracle. —SARK

Let Us Now Praise the Digital Camera

The advent of the digital camera has made photography an even easier and more accessible medium for recording our lives than ever before. With its instant viewing availability and deletion capabilities, digital photography has made every man, woman, and child feel that picture taking is not only easy, but totally essential for any moment. Carrying a digital camera with you wherever you go is a great way to pay attention. Why not take it with you to work?

TRY THIS

A good way to shake up the way you view your work world is to study one ordinary thing and collect it. One of the cool things about collecting something is the picture several objects can collectively create. Taking pictures of something as simple as the mugs your coworkers drink coffee out of every morning can create an interesting image of your office and its inhabitants.

Some other collectable images could include: coffee mugs on people's desks, people's hands, office plants, office art, photos on or around people's desks, and your work buddies' lunches.

Take pictures of your coworkers' shoes. This is an excellent way to engage with your coworkers. Suddenly, it's not just a Tuesday morning! It's a morning when Phil came by to take a picture of my green and brown penny loafers! It's a way to be in cahoots with your coworkers. When people ask you what it's for, say, "I'm working on an art project." That will make you sound totally interesting (and by the way, *you are*) and people will feel they are part of something grand. Most people love the attention and will be totally delighted. Be prepared for the occasional "no"—it will happen, but just move on to the next pair.

Other ideas for photography projects: self-portraits at 9 a.m. and 5 p.m. every day or five things you find beautiful at work. Go for it!

PO' GIRL'S MOCHA

when $4.50 at Starbucks is just too much

⊛ <u>INGREDIENTS</u> (FOUND IN MOST OFFICE KITCHENS AND/OR COFFEE ROOMS)

PLAIN OL' COFFEE +

SINGLE SERVING PACKET OF HOT CHOCOLATE! +

Half & Half!

① EMPTY CONTENTS OF HOT CHOCOLATE POWDER! (INTO A CUP, THAT IS)

② FILL CUP WITH COFFEE!

③ ADD 1/2 + 1/2 TO TASTE

④ STIR!

IT'S TASTY!

& Voilà!

IT'S TOTALLY FREE!

Make an Instructional Flier

YOU WILL NEED:

paper and pens, or computer and printer

Every job environment is unique and filled with its own rules, social norms, and tasks. If asked, how would you explain an activity or task you did during the day? Make a flier that spells out instructions for something simple and daily at work. Instead of the usual angry "Wash your cup!" sign left anonymously for coworkers who leave their dirty cups in the communal sink, how about creating a "How to Wash a Cup" flier?

Other Examples

* How to Write a Memo
* How to Give Good Table Service (for waiters and waitresses)
* How to Write a Report
* Casual Fridays: The Dos and Don'ts

Type it and/or illustrate it in step-by-step instructions. Then post it!

Create a New View ~

Carolyn See, in her excellent book *Making a Literary Life*, described how the writer Kay Boyle created a view and then wrote herself there.

Boyle grew up in Ohio, dreaming of living in Paris. While at grad school in New York, she married the first Frenchman she met and moved to France. There were only a few problems: The Frenchman was a tire salesman who moved them to a small town in France. It wasn't Paris, and their room in the small town had no windows. Boyle literally painted windows on her walls, thus creating a view. Then she wrote stories and wrote to every writer she knew of in Paris, introducing herself and paving the way toward the community and life of her dreams. She first created the view and then wrote herself to Paris, leaving the tire salesman and the windowless room behind.

In your cubicle, office, locker, or somewhere you can see it at work, put up a small picture of a window as a reminder that you are creating a new view for yourself. Consider your working life like Boyle's windowless room and your little makeshift window as the porthole to your city of lights.

CRISPY RICE CEREAL BARS

INGREDIENTS

- ¼ c. butter or margarine
- 1 10oz. Package of marshmallows
- ½ tsp. vanilla extract
- 6 c. Crispy rice Cereal

Crispy Rice Cereal

NOT JUST FOR BREAKFAST ANYMORE!

① In a large saucepan or double boiler, melt butter & marshmallows over low heat.

② Add Vanilla.

③ Remove from heat and add the crispy rice cereal — stirring constantly.

④ Using a greased rubber spatula, press mixture into a lightly greased baking pan.

⑤ Let cool & then cut into squares.

I'M YUMMY!

Food for the Masses

Make a treat for your coworkers. If you can, do something totally unexpected like making a pie or cake. Or even better: Make crispy rice cereal marshmallow treats. When was the last time you had some of those? Probably as long ago as any of your coworkers, too. People will be totally delighted!

Something to consider: One thing nobody ever thinks to bring to work is a veggie platter. I know, a veggie platter makes it sound like you're the house that passed out pencils at Halloween, but think about all the crap that is passed out at work for "treats." Once, my boss brought in a veggie platter with dip, and you'd have thought it was the most exotic, delicious thing there was. People were thrilled with a healthy, fresh snack for a change.

Discover the Mysteries of Your Mind

YOU WILL NEED:

notebook, journal, or sketchbook
scissors, tape, and/or glue

Go through your pads of paper, Post-its, or whatever has your little squiggles or drawings that you make when you are on the phone. Collect all your phone doodles and assemble them in a sketchbook. When the sketchbook is filled you'll be surprised by what you find!

Other Smaller Actions That Help

WEAR YOUR FAVORITE OUTFIT OR ITEM TO WORK. THIS CAN BE AS MINIMAL AS A PAIR OF RED SOCKS. BE SURE IT'S SOMETHING THAT MAKES YOU FEEL POWERFUL OR INSPIRED.

DRINK YOUR COFFEE OR TEA IN A CUP AND SAUCER.

EAT CHOCOLATE EVERYDAY AT 3PM.

FLOWERS (FOR YOU OR SOMEONE ELSE) ALWAYS HELP.

READ A POEM. IT TAKES FIVE MINUTES, BUT THE HEART WILL REMEMBER WONDER!

You will Enjoy Coming to Work!

For a long time it seemed to me that life was about to begin — real life. But there was always some obstacle in the way, something to be gotten through first, some unfinished business, time still to be served, a debt to be paid. At last it dawned on me that these obstacles were my life.

— Souza

These Obstacles Are Your Life

A number of years ago, I went through a period where I was so creatively blocked that I was convinced that I was either a tragic genius who had been used up too soon or a tragic genius that might die before her real talent ever truly blossomed. (If you surmise that while I was blocked, my ego was having a field day, you surmise correctly.) To cure my block I spent almost all my time "getting inspired" by reading inspiration books, creative blogs, memoirs, and biographies of artists, and watching movies about the artist's life. When not reading or watching "inspiring work" I'd prepare my work space. When not preparing my work space, I'd think, *Well, I just need to read one more book, you know, to get me in the mood.* I kept thinking that if I just had more inspiration, more research, more space, more *something*, then I'd be ready to create the magnificent work of my life. It's like I was waiting for my real life to begin so that I could be the person I dreamed of being. Like Father Alfred D. Souza said, one day it finally occurred to me that all this preparing, yearning, watching, and reading *was* my life.

I've known writers who have spent five years researching their novels, while never actually writing their novels. I've known painters who just needed the "right" space in order to do any painting. I've also known actors who knew they would be great if given the chance—the chance to do what? Act.

Give Yourself a Chance to Act!

Researching, preparing, or dreaming are all key parts of living the creative life, but like any career, if we want to make a living doing art, we must eventually move beyond this first step, and take small, concrete actions. For some of us, that may mean simply beginning to make art. For others, it may be to start getting our work *out there*. Taking action on whatever that *next* step you need to take has real power. It can not only change the way you approach your creative work, but it can give you a sense of real possibility. Anything *can* happen—as long as you take a single step on your own behalf.

TRY THIS

What is that next step that you have been avoiding? Is it writing a scene for your novel? Taking that pottery class? Picking up the guitar? Writing it down and making it visible can give light (and energy) toward taking that next step.

TRY THIS

Write a list of things you could do toward your creative work or ideal life that would take ten to fifteen minutes.

Examples: Write for fifteen minutes, research agents for fifteen minutes, sketch your right shoe, find the name of one literary journal, find a dance class.

Don't think about making art, just get it done. Let everyone else decide if it's good or bad, whether they love it or hate it. While they are deciding, make even more art.

- Andy Warhol

"But I Don't Have Time!"
(AND OTHER CRIES FROM THE HEART)

A friend of mine, a very gifted writer, once sat at lunch with me bemoaning the situation of his life. He was bored in his job; he liked his apartment, but he'd been there too long; he was ambivalent about the relationship he was in. Most important, he wasn't writing. He was considering something drastic: quitting everything and moving temporarily across the country to the West Coast.

I made the cardinal mistake of trying to be helpful. I asked him if he'd thought about joining a writing group or even taking a class—two things that can give a writer accountability, structure, and a sense of connection.

Man, was *that* annoying!

"You don't understand," he said. "I don't have time—I work a full-time job and I want *a life*."

"What about writing for fifteen minutes a day?" I asked. Again, I seemed to be the most annoying, not-getting-it person there was. "That's not the point," he said. "I want to *write*." Then he changed the subject, because *obviously* I did not understand the severity of his plight.

The thing was, I *did* understand. Like I said, I have been very creative about preparing my life as an artist, but I had a hard time actually ever doing art. I have a history of plotting escape routes, blowing up my life, and being utterly convinced that something huge and dramatic would need to change for me to find any sort of comfort and happiness in order to do my work.

There are plenty of reasons to blow up your life: You want adventure; you hate your job; you are bored with your town, your relationship, and/or your whole life. The basic desire: YOU WANT CHANGE. This is all understandable, but ask yourself this before making any huge choices in the name of your creative life: *What will be different? What will change besides circumstance?*

It took me years to realize that I could do all kinds of drastic acts like quitting jobs, relationships, towns (or all of the above), but what showed up at the next job, relationship, and town was still *me*. In all creative lives, risk is important— but ask yourself, how does it feel to do your art in the life you have right now? If it seems impossible to do now, what will really change with where you are later?

The Bad News: If you can't do your art—even a little—in the life you have now, with the person you are right this second, YOU MAY NEVER DO IT.

The Good News: You are PERFECT! You don't have to change anything about yourself or your situation to start doing your work *now*.

Ways to Find Time

So when, oh when, do you get all this art stuff done? It's a lot of work just getting up and going to work, so how do you find time to do your creative work and still have a life?

Answer: Priorities, priorities.

Whether we realize it or not, all of us live according to our priorities. We keep down jobs because we have made it a priority to do so. We watch a particular TV show because the pleasure we get from it (or the ease of it) is a priority. Like the conversation I had with my friend, who had a very full life, writing was not quite (*yet*) a priority. There is nothing wrong with this at all, except for that pesky yearning. Damn that yearning! Why can't it shut up already? Unfortunately, if we don't make our creative careers a priority, that yearning can turn into things like anger and jealousy.

TRY THIS

The hard truth: If something is a priority we make time. Sometimes it's a matter of shifting our priorities in order to make room for what we yearn to do.

What Are Your Priorities?

Write a list of things you always put first. Your job, a good night's sleep, your kid's lunches, and so forth. Whatever you put ahead of anything else.

Extra Credit

Pick one item on that list and for one day put it on the back burner. Call in healthy to work, stay up late or get up early, buy lunch for your kid on the way to school. Sometimes just allowing a shift in priorities can open a whole window of time!

Ways to Find Time: "Small Moves, Ellie. Small Moves."

Probably one of the biggest struggles to getting creative work done is the belief that it has to be *significant* in order to amount to anything. It all feels so *large* that we believe that we need big swaths of time and/or space in order to live out our dreams. No one seems to take into account that all large and significant works are actually an accumulation of small actions and individual pieces of material. Think about a skyscraper: Sure, it's enormous, monumental, and takes a long time to make. Yet, among all that, someone spent time drilling in small screws so that larger screws could be added so that even larger metal beams could be built and so on. We see the skyscraper, but we don't see the tiny items and gestures that made it rise. In the same way, when we see novels, we don't see the single page. When we see a painting in a museum, we don't see the millions of brushstrokes that created the whole of the picture.

> *Fantasizing about pursuing our art full-time,*
> *we fail to pursue it part-time—or at all.*
> —Julia Cameron

Reducing your expectations and making small moves every day can be tremendously productive. The Pulitzer Prize-winning author Carol Shields was a mother of five when she began to write. She made a promise to herself—if she could just get one or two pages of handwritten manuscript done a day, no matter what, that was enough. She stuck to her writing "schedule" and in nine months had a draft of her first novel.

TRY THIS

Using your list of fifteen-minute actions—take action now! No matter the state of your home, your day, your life, give yourself fifteen minutes *right now* to do your creative work. **Do it!**

Reminder: It doesn't take much to do more than nothing. Fifteen minutes today is fifteen minutes more than yesterday. One page today is one page more than yesterday.

WARNING

One of the total bummers that I discovered upon actually acting on my creative work was that it wasn't instantly fantastic.

If you have a sneaking feeling that your work is totally bad or boring or not what you dreamed of it being, forgive yourself and keep doing it.

In the beginning, the act of doing your work—whatever it is—is the only outcome you should be worried about. Practice tenderness toward yourself just for the act of transcending your procrastination, blocks, or whatever has stopped you in the past.

YOU DID IT! Keep going!

Every Move Counts

I meet with a group of women once a month so that we can support each other in making changes in our lives. Every single month we set goals for what we would like to accomplish in the next month. In the beginning, during check-ins, there always seemed to be a moment when members of the group would sheepishly admit, "Well, I didn't do all the things I said I would do." And you could tell there was this weight of guilt on them. Finally I asked, "Well, what *did* you get done?" There were always some aspects of the goal that got accomplished, but the member was discounting them because it wasn't *all* of the goal. I have come to believe that even if it's one out of three, it's still one more than zero. Small gestures matter— and it's high time we start recognizing what we do instead of what we don't do. We do a disservice to ourselves by not acknowledging even the smallest things we *do* accomplish. As the author and artist Keri Smith reminds us, "Something is better than nothing." Amen!

TRY THIS

What are some of the things you've done toward your goals?

Examples: Reading this book and doing your work for fifteen minutes.

Ways to Find Time: The Basics

Note: None of these are original, but all of them work!

Limit television, the black hole of passivity (and I say this with love). I don't own a TV, not because I am against or above it, but because if I owned one, *I'd never stop watching*. This is one of the keys to my productivity. If you are not willing to get rid of your TV (and who is?), limit your TV use. Have at least one TV-free night, by not only turning it off, but *covering it up*. Put a scarf, piece of fabric, or blanket over your TV. Notice how this changes the vibe of your entire home.

Limit Internet. It's just interactive television—and don't try to tell me any different! How many times do you go to check your email and end up sitting there for an hour or more browsing? Have Internet-free nights or entire weekends. Unplug it! Consign all of your Internet activity to the office (you know you check it there, anyway). If necessary, disconnect the Internet at home entirely.

Get up an hour earlier or stay up an hour later. Depending on whether you are most productive in the morning or at night, try curbing your sleep schedule by one hour. This really can help! I know, I know—let's be real: It can be hard to get

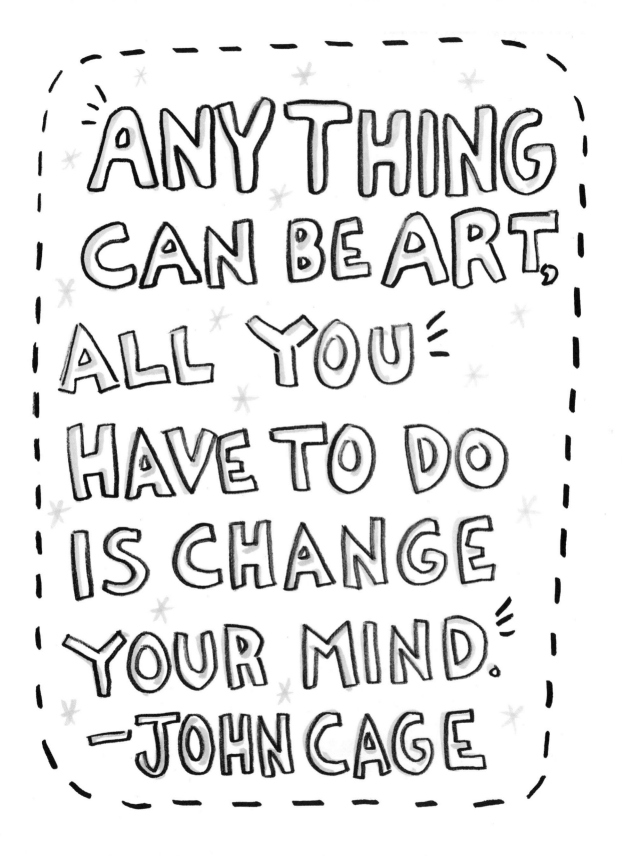

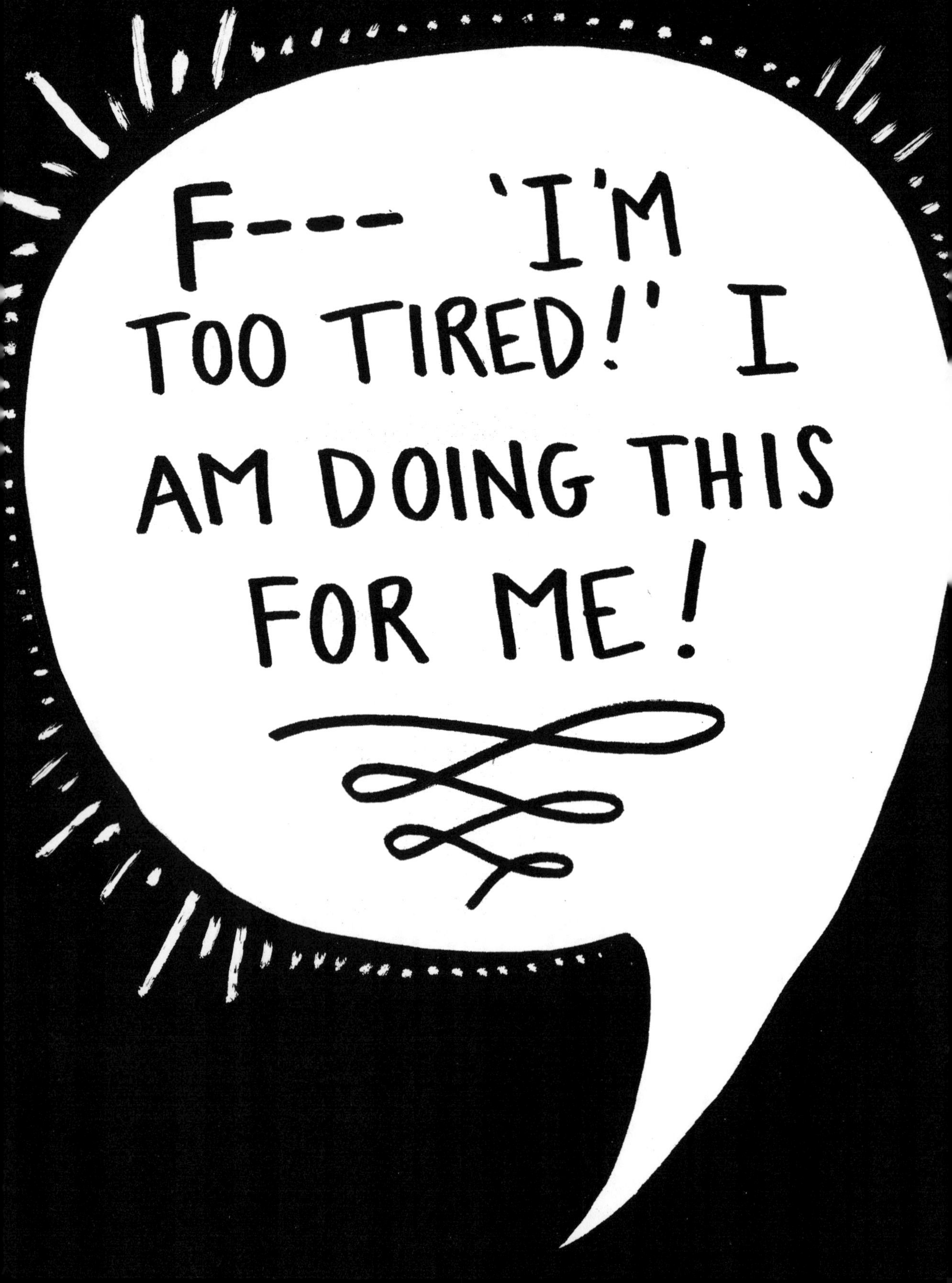
F--- 'I'M TOO TIRED!' I AM DOING THIS FOR ME!

up early or be motivated after a full day of work. You think, "But I'm too tired." To this, I recommend what Michael Filan, painter and teacher, often declares out loud in such moments: **"FUCK 'I'M TOO TIRED'! I AM DOING THIS FOR ME!"** It's particularly potent if you're feeling numb and you're thinking passive thoughts like, "Oh, I'll do it later," or "I'm not in the mood." Say it out loud! Often what will happen once you get started is that you will be filled with energy!

Go to work early. I used to have a job where I arrived at 6 a.m. every day to write for two hours before the day began. What worked about this was that it gave me space and quiet to focus before my day began (and I was never late to work!).

Stay at work late. I know a number of writers and artists who do this in order to find time to create. Like the early option, it keeps you away from the distractions at home and gives you a specific time and space for your work.

Remember lunchtime adventures. What can you do during lunch? Even one lunch hour a week spent writing, drawing, photographing, researching, mailing letters, anything artistic is one hour more than you did yesterday.

Do your work during the workday. My friend Felicia Sullivan wrote her beautiful memoir, *The Sky Isn't Visible From Here*, almost entirely at work. Note: She also got all of her work done and won awards and bonuses for the job she was doing. *Do not* do your creative work on the job if it stops you from getting your job done or causes trouble.

Schedule it in. In order to schedule in writing time, the writer Natalie Goldberg has sometimes called a friend and left a message: "I will be at the café writing on Sunday at 3 p.m., if you want to join me—but don't call and tell me if you're coming or not." This way, on the off chance that her friend did join her, Goldberg was forced to keep the appointment even if she didn't feel like writing. Make an appointment in your calendar, BlackBerry, or computer for your creative work: *Wednesday evenings from 6:00 p.m. to 7:00 p.m. I will create or do something toward my artistic life/career.*

Take a class. Taking a class in what you are interested in helps schedule it automatically. When I was working full-time and performing as a musician, I took a painting class to preserve my visual art as a living presence in my life. Otherwise, I'd never have had time for it.

Feelings TO EXPECT WHEN YOU Actually GET TO WORK ON YOUR Creative DREAM:

IMPATIENT!   ELATED!

anxious!   BORED!

INSPIRED!   Hopeful!

Tired!   Encouraged!

FRUSTRATED!   Hungry!

nauseated!   WORRIED!

HAPPY!   Terrified!

Blissed Out!   DISCOURAGED!

YOU NAME IT, You Feel IT!

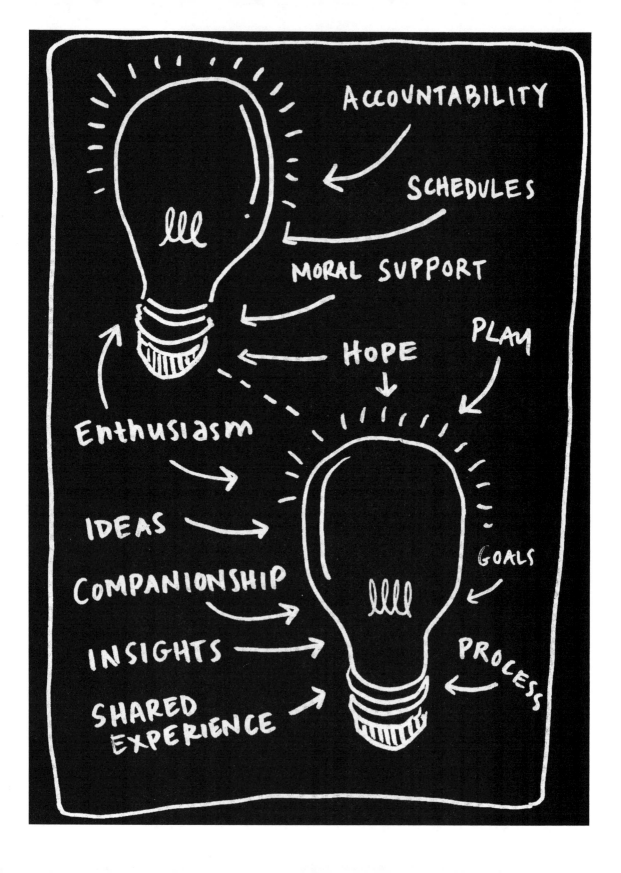

Groups, Partnerships, and Collaborators

We Can Do It!

I used to be a very solitary artist. I was fiercely independent, and it somehow fed the fiery belief that I was *real* and *original* and *deep* (oh yes, that argument again). Yet, as I got older and realized the things I actually want in my life, I felt increasingly isolated and stuck in my own vacuum. I wasn't getting as much done as I wanted, and I was also getting stuck in my head about the *idea* of being an artist and not so much being an *active* artist. The reality is, I need accountability, a schedule, and most of all, I need other people to get things done.

So now I am part of two fantastic, productive groups: a writing group and a creative action group. As a result, I've not only been writing fiction again but also finishing short stories, getting critical feedback about them, and revising them. I also have been making small concrete moves toward my goals, like submitting these stories to literary journals, thanks to the support and accountability of three other women in my creative group.

If you want to get things done but are having a hard time actually doing them, nothing can be better than forming or joining a group of like-minded people. Suddenly, it isn't just

JOHN MAYNARD KEYNES — ECONO-MIST

LYTTON STRACHEY — WRITER

E.M. FORSTER — WRITER

CLIVE BELL — CRITIC

VANESSA BELL — ARTIST

DUNCAN GRANT — ARTIST

LEONARD WOOLF — CRITIC, WRITER + PUBLISHER

VIRGINIA WOOLF — WRITER

ROGER FRY — ARTIST

members of the Bloomsbury Group

about you in your small world who cares abo

somebody else is in cahoots. A sense of comm

It can be the difference between *wishing* and *do*

If you don't like the idea of a group, thin

collaboration. Who would you like to collaborate v

Some groups are legendary!

Collaborations and groups have been shaping the art world for a long time. Consider the Bloomsbury Group, which fostered and launched the famous careers of writers Virginia Woolf and Lytton Strachey, as well as the painters Vanessa Bell and Roger Fry and the economist John Maynard Keynes. What began as a regular evening of conversations on art and life launched the careers of people who challenged the world of literature, English society, and art. They went to each other's art openings, published one another, painted each other, and supported each other's efforts. Without the support of the group, many members might not have created or flourished at all. But together, they were a powerful posse.

Some Guidelines to Keep in Mind for Groups or Partnerships
   * All members must be active or ready to start taking action in whatever endeavor they want to pursue. It will become apparent pretty early on who wants to actually do and who wants to just talk about it. If it becomes clear that someone isn't really ready to make constructive

moves, withhold judgment and let them go. They will figure it out and so will you!

* **Have regularly scheduled meetings.** Do not waste your time trying to schedule each meeting to meet the schedule of every member—it will be a perfect opportunity for people to feel "too busy." We all have busy lives so why not have a specific time and date already in the calendar, like the third Thursday of every month? Psychologically, this works like a bookmark for the brain. You will come to expect and work for the regularly scheduled time. Meeting a minimum of once a month is recommended. If you meet less frequently, your goals, ideas, and sense of accomplishment will go out the door. Ideally, once a week would be great—but not many of us have that kind of time.

* **Each member must have clear and defined goals—even if they are minute.** Remember: No goal is too small! In my creative group, we each set goals from cleaning our closets to taking a sewing class.

* **Have a system for accountability.** If you are meeting once a month, how about an email check-in with the group every two weeks? This keeps people actively engaged in their process throughout the month. Or better yet, have a system where people email the group once they've accomplished a goal. Nobody needs to respond to this

email, but it is like an invisible meeting that says, "I did this and you saw me do this." Accountability is key.

* **Keep the focus on what is getting accomplished.** Every move counts! Remember to focus on what is accomplished instead of what isn't. Just because you researched a class, but didn't have time to sign up for it, doesn't mean nothing was accomplished. Members can always redefine goals at meetings and make the next month's goal following up on actions already made. The point is to get into the habit of acknowledging the efforts that we do make, so that we don't get stopped midway by hopeless thinking. Something *is* always better than nothing.

* **Limit bitching and gossiping.** This is especially important if you are meeting with people from work. If needed, schedule five minutes tops for people to talk about their lives and then move on. Keep the focus on what you want to happen, not what you don't.

GROUPS DO IT TOGETHER!

Don't Forget Time Off

We work a minimum of two jobs—that's a lot of work! As creative types with a day job, weekends or other "days off" are immediately reserved for our creative work.

Our creative work is considered downtime—but it is not.

While I am encouraging you to continue your creative work in spite of your day job, it is important to provide yourself with *real* downtime, too! Not that long ago, it occurred to me that there were no things I did simply for pleasure. I had this attitude that all my activities had to have *meaning* or why bother? But my seriousness was burning me out. When I didn't take a break, I tended to get blocked and to be *totally uptight*. Now I make sure to have at least one day every week where I don't do anything "serious" or "artistic." It turns out that even non-artistic things, like having a social life or baking a pie, do have meaning. Pleasure and play are just as important.

A word about procrastination: Sometimes, in order to give ourselves downtime we procrastinate on our creative work, losing hours or days (or years) to dawdling or avoiding. Here's the catch, though: PROCRASTINATION IS NOT DOWNTIME. Procrastination takes a lot of energy and leads to guilt and critical self-talk. It's a better use of time to do the work and then give yourself a break! You deserve it.

TRY THIS

Write a list of twenty things that give you pleasure.

Now do one of them. It will be a pleasure!

DO YOU RECALL, FROM YOUR CHILDHOOD ON, HOW VERY MUCH THIS LIFE OF YOURS HAS LONGED FOR GREATNESS? I SEE IT NOW, HOW FROM THE VANTAGE POINT OF GREATNESS IT LONGS FOR EVEN GREATER GREATNESS. THAT IS WHY IT DOES NOT LET UP BEING DIFFICULT, BUT THAT IS ALSO WHY IT WILL NOT CEASE TO GROW.

—Rainer Maria Rilke

"I've Wasted My Life!"
"It's Too Late!"
"I've Lost So Much Time!"

We've all thought variations of these beliefs at one time or another about dreams we haven't lived, goals we haven't accomplished, or ways in which we wish our lives were, but aren't. The truth is no matter what we have accomplished or haven't, we have been living full lives. It's hard to see this when we are face-to-face with something we feel is missing.

I've wanted to go back to Paris for fifteen years, and I sometimes beat myself up for not going and wonder why the heck I haven't accomplished this dream that seems so easy for others to do. I see the FIFTEEN YEARS in looming large letters and followed by "And I *still* haven't done it." A quick cure is to write a list of things you've done *instead* of whatever you think you've put off or haven't yet done.

For me that would include going to college, moving across the country five times, reading countless books, taking a writing class with my favorite writer, painting pictures, and touring California and New England as a musician.

TRY THIS

List dreams and goals that you've wanted to do, but haven't.

TRY THIS

What have you done *instead* of doing these things? Taken jobs? Eaten ice cream? Accomplished something else?

Your life is not a waste!

We are filled with rich experiences and accomplishments. Claiming them helps ease the pressure we put on ourselves for not choosing to do something we could still go after.

TRY THIS

If you believe you are wasting your life, here is a great way to feel useful and empowered in your life right now: Write a list of *everything* you've done in the last six months. What movies have you seen or books have you read? How many hours have you worked? Did you fill any journals, draw any pictures, or take any trips? This is a simple way to instantly see how your life is full and that you are actively participating in it. If six months is too overwhelming, try covering a single month. The point of this exercise is to own your time and see that you are alive and kicking!

TRY THIS

Now write a list of things you'd *like* to do in the next six months. This could be everything from what you hope for or the simple things that you want to accomplish. This is a great place to plant the seeds for what you want to grow. Also, you never know what will grow when you actively acknowledge what you want. Dream big *and* small!

Examples: I want to go see the Van Gogh exhibit, send out two more stories, and have a kick-ass birthday.

TRY THIS

Now write a list of things you'd *like* to do in the next six months. This could be everything from what you hope for or the simple things that you want to accomplish. This is a great place to plant the seeds for what you want to grow. Also, you never know what will grow when you actively acknowledge what you want. Dream big *and* small!

Examples: I want to go see the Van Gogh exhibit, send out two more stories, and have a kick-ass birthday.

Your life is not a waste!

We are filled with rich experiences and accomplishments. Claiming them helps ease the pressure we put on ourselves for not choosing to do something we could still go after.

TRY THIS

If you believe you are wasting your life, here is a great way to feel useful and empowered in your life right now: Write a list of *everything* you've done in the last six months. What movies have you seen or books have you read? How many hours have you worked? Did you fill any journals, draw any pictures, or take any trips? This is a simple way to instantly see how your life is full and that you are actively participating in it. If six months is too overwhelming, try covering a single month. The point of this exercise is to own your time and see that you are alive and kicking!

HE HAS WRITTEN MANY AMAZING SONGS ABOUT HIS VARIOUS DAY JOBS AS A BARTENDER, DAY LABORER, AND TRUCK DRIVER.

HAMELL ON TRIAL

Once, while I was living in California, I wrote in my "next six months" list that I wanted to connect with an artist I admired. I had in mind the writer and artist Lynda Barry, but what I got was the singer/songwriter Ed Hamell of Hamell on Trial. He's somebody I've admired for years and he just "happened" to be playing a show in the next town. On a whim my friend and I spontaneously invited him to have ice cream with us after the show. I was totally beside myself when he accepted. We ended up having an inspiring talk about art, music, life, and location. He was one of the earliest voices that encouraged me to move to New York. (Thanks, Ed!)

I Still Feel Stuck, I Can't I Can't I Can't, or The Big What If

Sometimes no matter what you read, or what a friend says, or what you have previously known or not known, you still feel screwed and stuck and don't have a clue how to move forward. I went through a period of time when I wasn't sure I'd ever write a song again or be able to continue what I considered THE ARTISTIC ENDEAVOR of my life: music. It was a painful and confusing period, where I was ravaged by anxiety and the big questions: *What if I never get back on the horse again? What if I'm washed up? Why can't I just move on and get going? What is wrong with me?* Whether I knew it or not, I was driving myself crazy with the constant fretting and questioning and it was keeping me from taking any action and moving on.

The problem with worry, like procrastination, is that it keeps you *very busy*, while never actually producing anything. We think worry helps because we believe it will somehow answer or prepare us for the outcome of our problems, but in fact, it just keeps us stymied and occupied with more problems. We want to force the problems and the questions away, but sometimes that can only make the pain and worry worse.

The simple truth I wish I had known when I was up to my eyeballs in these questions? The struggle can feel like the whole picture, but it's really just *part* of the process. I am here to tell you that it is totally normal to have feelings of serious doubt, and the trick is not to identify yourself with the pain and questions completely.

I remember there was a batch of chicken eggs being incubated under an orange heat lamp in my kindergarten classroom. We couldn't wait to see them hatch. Then, one morning, when we all witnessed the first chick chipping away, we gathered around mesmerized for about one minute. When it became apparent that this wasn't happening nearly fast enough to meet our five-year-old excitement, somebody said, "Maybe we should help it?" But the teacher explained to us that if we did, the chick would die. The chipping through the egg was part of its growing up.

Consider your anxiety like an impatient five-year-old and the big questions like those baby birds. They need time to make their way out of the dark. Fussing over them with worry, or making choices out of anxiety, will often do more damage than help.

TRY THIS

For six months ignore the engine of worry and get to work. When you find yourself wringing your hands over questions like *Will I ever accomplish my goals? Am I really a writer or an actress?* or *Why can't I figure it all out now?*—just STOP. Say it out loud: "Stop!" or "Part of the process!" or "Just because I feel it, it doesn't mean it's true!" And then get back to work. Do what you can for fifteen minutes, or write a list of what you want to do specifically, and break that down into fifteen-minute actions. Break the spell of worry and make an effort. If you are still worried when that six months is over, give it another six months.

Lather, rinse, and repeat.

Looking for Work and Other Adventures

When we set out to find our "dream jobs" we tend to look at money, convenience, titles, or industry, but never what kind of people we are or what lives we actually want to live. Rarely do we look for jobs that support the life we want. We instead arrange our lives to support the job we get. We buy clothes we don't like to wear, commute long distances, work long hours, and spend time with people we normally wouldn't choose to be with. This is fine if it's what you want, but if it hinders you from other things like creating and a social life, then stagnation, boredom, and resentment set in.

Acknowledging who we are and what kinds of lives we want to live doesn't necessarily mean quitting the administrative job to work in a gallery (although it could). It means asking yourself: What is it that you want to live?

My friend Richard is a writer who has worked in a bookstore for over a decade. Though it doesn't pay as much as an office job, the bookstore complements his life: It puts Richard, an outgoing person, in contact with books and authors he loves, and offers him a discount and a flexible schedule so that he can write and have a social life. Since it has a casual atmosphere, he can wear whatever he wants and can mentally leave at the end of his shift, allowing his time off to be his own.

What does your ideal life look like? How would you be spending your time? Where would you live? Would you get up early? Stay up late? Would you have a social atmosphere or would you like to be more alone? What do you wear? Who are you with? Who do you know? Do you drive, walk, take the train? The more specific the better! Ideal life lists are like maps telling us where to go.

MANY PEOPLE BELIEVE THAT CYNICISM IS THE HEIGHT OF COURAGE. ACTUALLY, CYN-ICISM IS THE HEIGHT OF COWARDICE. IT IS INNO-CENCE AND OPEN-HEART-EDNESS THAT REQUIRES THE TRUE COURAGE - HOWEVER OFTEN WE ARE HURT AS A RESULT OF IT.   - ERICA JONG

Some Tips for Job Searching

Before you look for another job or make any real changes, ask yourself, *What do I want?* (as opposed to what you don't want).

When we want to leave a situation, we tend to think in negatives: *I don't want to work in an office, I don't want a place that doesn't appreciate me,* and so forth. It's actually not that productive to look for a job or make a change with a list of things you don't want hanging over your head. The more specific you are about what you *do* want, the better the chances of getting what you want.

Note: This may be harder to do than you think. We have been so conditioned to focus on what doesn't work that it takes some adjusting to know what does work. If you're having a hard time, then make positives out of your list of negatives.

Example: "I don't want to work in an office" can be turned into "I want to work in a creative environment" or "I want to work from home." The more specific you are, the better.

TRY THIS

What are your actual needs? Don't forget that you already have a job as an artist! Sure, you need to pay the rent, but you will need time to do artistic work and time to play and relax. What else will you need? In Part One I asked you to write a list of what your job provides for you. What will your ideal job provide for you?

A helpful reminder when looking for work:

YOU ARE WELCOME EVERYWHERE.

I read this phrase in one of the artist/writer SARK's books awhile back, and I have come to realize that nothing better can be said to you when you are looking for work. It's 100 percent true—you *are* welcome everywhere. This is so hard to remember when you are sending out query letters and polishing your résumé. It can feel like you are the beggar at the door, but you are not. The workforce needs you and if you approach it like you are the supplier instead of the needy, doors will open to you everywhere.

This is also a perfect reminder for anyone sending out stories, auditioning, trying to get gigs, anything that is requiring you to stretch, to try, to put yourself in the face of rejection. Seriously, you are welcome everywhere.

Essential Abundance
~The Bare Minimum on Money

Okay, okay, let's get down to the *nitty gritty*. Let's talk about the reality of money.

We all have lots of ideas about what money is. We think money is the answer to our problems, but our thinking about money can also be the source of some of our problems. We equate money with a means for pleasure, and yet we put making money in front of creating or experiencing pleasure. We think in amounts of money, but not in terms of sanity or joy. For some of us, having lots of money might mean "the good life," but we never ask ourselves, *What does that "good life" look like SPECIFICALLY?*

TRY THIS

What does the "good life" look like to you specifically?

TRY THIS

What is money to you? When you think of having money, what does it mean to you in your life as it is now? Does it mean freedom? Power? Grist for the mill? What?

TRY THIS

What else gives you the feeling of having money?

Example: For me, having money means a sense of ease. What else gives me a sense of ease? Wearing jeans, lazy mornings, going for walks, and paying my bills on time.

Finding Your Essential Abundance

Often, what we want from monetary wealth is really just a sense of abundance. But abundance is not about how much money you have, it's about how much you are enjoying your life.

I don't make much money, but I live a very rich life. This is possible because I know what gives me joy and meaning and that is where my energy goes. It doesn't mean I don't get stuck or fearful, but I know the minimum of what I need to feel secure and abundant. I know I need rent, a good home life, and time to do my art. That's the bare minimum. Everything else is just icing on the cake—and I love icing.

strong
coffee and
half & half

HOOD
half & half

I love
it!

TRY THIS

What are things that give you joy? List twenty things from
the simple, like "staying home on a rainy day," to the ornate,
like "walking in Paris."

Now, how much money does each cost?

Keep Out the Spirit of Poverty

Luxury is not a necessity to me,

but beautiful and good things are.

—Anaïs Nin

It's important to realize that minimal things can bring on the feeling of abundance, no matter what you have (or don't have) in the ol' checking account. Sometimes there is just one simple thing that can make you feel a sense of well-being. For me the minimum is good coffee. I never feel "poor" when I have good coffee in the house.

What are the things that make you feel abundance? Is it a clean house? A nice pair of red socks? Fresh flowers? For my friend Rick, it's a bottle of real maple syrup. As long as he has that he can't feel broke—he can have real maple syrup.

TRY THIS

List ten things that give you a feeling of well-being.

When You Are Feeling Fearful About Money

* FIND A WAY TO INCREASE YOUR WELL-BEING: Take a bath, light candles, etc.

* Bake or cook something. The physical act of chopping or measuring will calm you. The smell will transport you.

* WRITE A LIST OF REASONS WHY YOU CAN SUCCEED.

* KNOW THAT IT WILL PASS — ONE DAY YOU WILL WAKE-UP AND BE IN A NEW EXPERIENCE!

* Do a "problem solving" activity like going for a walk, writing, sewing, cleaning — anything repetitive & "mindless."

* Nurture your physical space: clean & organize your home — it has healing properties!

You ♥ ARE ♥ SAFE!

Other Things That Help

Pay attention to your language. How many times do you say, "I am so broke"? Notice how these words affect you and how you interact with the world. Same with terms like "I can't afford it" or "things are tight." These words are often thrown around, but they have deeper meaning in our lives. They affect how we live out our lives. It may sound silly, but saying, "I choose not to do that right now" instead of "I can't afford it" has real power.

TRY THIS

The next time you feel tempted to make a comment about your financial affairs, stop and see how you physically feel. Check in with your body. I always feel heavy and trapped when I talk despairingly about money.

TRY THIS

Get rid of all the clothing and items in your home that make you feel shabby. We all have these things. For years I hung on to dresses that I bought for weddings or special events because they were "nice" and in good condition. In reality, I couldn't stand these outfits and I avoided wearing them because they made me feel uncomfortable or "not me." The moment I gave them away, I felt a sense of release and energy I hadn't anticipated. It inspired me go through and get rid of books I didn't like and pictures that well-meaning family members gave me but I just didn't like. What this did was distill my life into the things that mattered most to me. My home felt instantly better!

Start a change jar. Scour your coats, pockets, sofa, and wallet for loose change and put it in a jar. Every time you have some extra change, add it to the jar. Mark the change jar with something that means something to you, like a hope, a wish, or a plan. I have one marked "Travel," because it acts like an easy depository for a traveling fund—something I dream of doing, but have a hard time planning for. My husband was bemoaning that he didn't have enough for savings when I pointed out the fact that he had collected three jars of change! He has had a habit of putting all his change in a jar for years. This is his unconscious savings plan. Every cent counts. A change jar can act as a physical reminder that you are always abundant and that you have enough!

PROBLEM SOLVING ACTIVITIES

Ways to calm your mind so that ideas and solutions will flow

DOING THE DISHES!

WALKING!

CLEANING!

WRITING IN YOUR JOURNAL OR NOTEBOOK!

COOKING!

ANYTHING REPETITIVE LIKE HAND SEWING, PUZZLES, DRAWING SPIRALS, OR DOODLING "MINDLESSLY"!

ALL YOUR PROBLEMS ARE TAKEN CARE OF

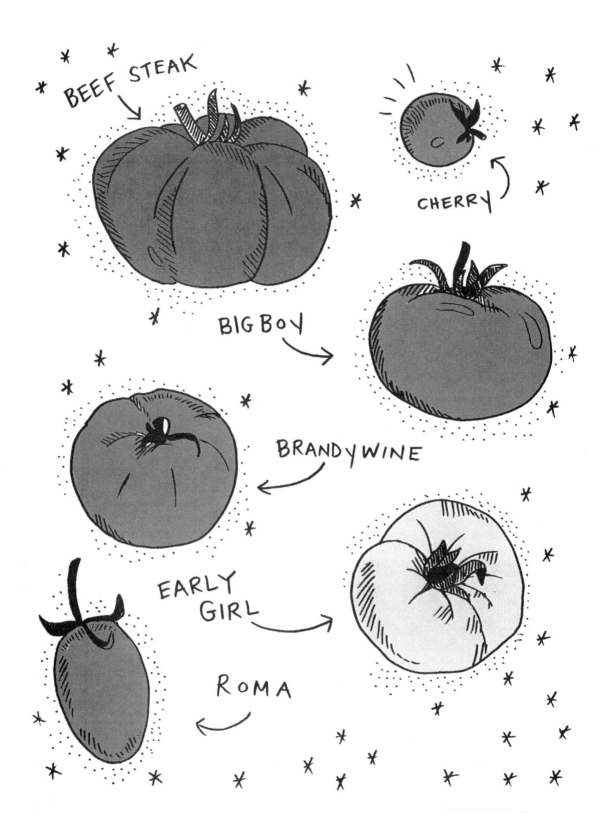

The Big Red Tomato in the Sky

For years I had this belief that tomatoes were too expensive for me—*tomatoes!* So I never bought them—yet, often they were cheaper than the milk I bought or the cereal I ate. What it really was about was believing that I couldn't have all that I wanted—even the easily attainable. I never did the simplest, empowering things, because I thought I had no money, even though I did have money. Then I'd (un)consciously spend on things like coffee at the café every day when I had good coffee at home and no tomatoes!

TRY THIS

Question your assumptions about money!
Fill in the blanks.

> When it comes to money I . . .
> I can't . . .
> I don't . . .
> I am not . . .
> I have . . .
> I am . . .
> I believe . . .

✳ Frugal ✳ Luxuries ✳

> **Luxuries are best experienced in small doses.**
> **—Stefan Sagmeister**

Before you dismiss me as Miss Frugality USA, let me be clear about abundance and money: I am not against luxury. Some of my favorite places to be are considered extravagant and luxurious. I still participate in and enjoy these things, while living on "less." The point of living abundantly is knowing what makes you truly happy and living those things more instead of filling up your life with the stuff you think you "need." Sometimes I think if only I could live in an apartment on the Upper West Side of Manhattan instead of Brooklyn, I would be really living! But I am not willing to work more hours in order to afford the rent (not to mention give up the amount of space I currently live in). My time is worth more than any apartment on the Upper West Side. I can always visit (and I do).

Consider this: What good is making money if you have no time to do your creative work or spend time with your family or anything else that gives you joy?

TRY THIS

Take a small notebook and for one week record every penny found or spent without judgment or worry. At the end of the week see what you spent your money on—this is a good indicator of what your priorities are and how you live with money. Again, this isn't about judgment or feeling guilty—it's only an exploration!

You will find this exercise in almost every money how-to book there is—and for good reason: It works! Few of us have any *clue* as to where our money *actually* goes. It's also a great way to gently explore money when we are afraid to even look.

Extra credit: Do it for a whole month.

This activity is about more than getting your checkbook balanced. It's about discovering where your energy goes. I find when I am feeling stressed or out of control about money, it's because I have been struggling with something else and it's being expressed through the money I am spending. When I am happy and content, I tend to spend less.

TRY THIS

What do you express with money?

Some Thoughts on Debt

School, home, and personal loans, credit card debt, and other obligations—all created from transactions made under the assumption that if someone who has money fronts it, it will be paid back. We go into these agreements with abandon, trepidation, denial, and/or amusement. I remember signing away for my college loans with a secret belief that not only would I not be able to pay them back, but I wouldn't have to—HA! The joke was on me the moment the first bill arrived. Guess I better figure how to pay them back.

TRY THIS

Before you borrow somebody else's abundance with credit cards or loans, first check to see if you believe in your *own* abundance. **The next time you charge something, get a loan, or make a payment on a loan or charge, ask yourself:**

* Do I believe in my earning potential to pay this back?
* Do I believe that in purchasing this or borrowing this I am increasing my ability to earn enough to pay this back?

TRY THIS

The next time you pay rent or pay a bill or a debt, think about what you are paying for. So often we resent the checks we write for our bills, but in truth, it's an equal exchange of abundance. Next time you pay your electric bill, think about all the things that electricity supplies you with (TV, computer, reading light, etc.). A big thing that I always resented was paying my school loans. Now when I write checks to my school loan companies, I think about the things that college gave me that still exist in my life today: ongoing friendships, my love of literature, the ability to play guitar and write songs, and so on. Without the loans, I wouldn't have been able to attend that school. I am grateful for that experience.

Doing this breaks the feeling of being depleted of our money and recognizes that we get plenty in exchange for the checks we write.

START YOUR OWN EXCHANGE

FREE SOLUTIONS · FREE IDEAS

DINNER CLUBS!
POTLUCKS!

CLOTHING

CLOTHING SWAPS!

TRANS-
PORTATION

CAR POOL!

CHILD
CARE

BABYSITTING
TRADE!

ENTER-
TAINMENT

MOVIE GROUPS!

CULTURE

LECTURE
SERIES!

BOOK
CLUBS

DISCUSSION
GROUPS!

CONNECT WITH YOUR FAMILY, FRIENDS, AND COMMUNITY

The Whole Life Picture

I read a blog entry by a fellow part-time employee and artist that declared she never planned on working full-time again. She had burned out at her jobs and had a habit of leaving after a year or two. Now that she had found the balance in her life, she felt free to enjoy her job. A number of people left positive comments, but then the inevitable comment arrived from someone who said she envied anyone who could be financially able to work part-time and she should consider herself lucky.

This comment might have come from me a number of years ago. I remember reading similar blog entries by artists and feeling like they had somehow won the lottery. It filled me with so much yearning and pain.

What I want to say *now* to this commenter is that it isn't lucky or extravagant to make different choices. It just takes adjusting. Sometimes the first adjustment involves our ideas about how our lives work. When we question our assumptions about how things are, things we thought were "impossible" become more attainable.

Stop dividing your life up into separate parts of money, work, and play. Look at your life as one whole picture, knowing what you want out of life and arranging your life to support that vision. What are you currently supporting? Your life matters. Who will support it, if not you?

~ We Are All So Proud of You ~

The place in which I'll fit will not exist until I make it.

—James Baldwin

I have a dream that everyone—not just artists—will get up every day and feel empowered and encouraged by their own efforts in the world. Jobs are a way that we show up and participate, and so many of us feel bewildered by the roles we end up in. I wanted to write this book to tell you that, whether you like your job or not, you are seen and what you do matters. You have been making it work for a long time now, getting up, commuting in, spending time with people you normally wouldn't, wearing stiff clothing, and maintaining the status quo. Meanwhile you also steal time to paint after 5:00 p.m. or write before you wait tables on the late shift, or sew for another hour after your daughter is in bed. So many of us feel that our time is not ours. Let this book be a reminder that your time is always yours to claim, whether it means jumping ship entirely to gallivant around the world or for just a moment dancing in the mailroom when you see your coworker.

About two weeks before I moved to New York from a small town in California, I went to see the writer David Sedaris read. I was excited to move to New York, but scared about getting a job. Since I had enjoyed his writing about working in New York, I told Sedaris that I was scared about getting a job and finding my place in New York, and did he have any pointers? I expected him to laugh, but instead he looked at me seriously and asked, "How old are you?" I told him and he said immediately, "You're going to do fine."

"Really?"

"Yeah, I was the same age when I moved to New York. It was perfect. That city can eat people up, but you are going at the perfect time."

That is when he wrote in my book: *We are all so proud of you.*

So as you leave this book, on your way to the crazy buzzing city that is your life, let me leave you with this:

You're going to be fine.

Your timing is perfect.

And yes, we are all so proud of you.